LYON
Vacation Guide
2025

Discover Lyon: A Journey Through France's Culinary and Cultural Treasure in 2025

COPYRIGHT

No part of this book may be reproduced, distributed, or transmitted in any form or by any means, including photocopying, recording, or other electronic or mechanical methods, without the prior written permission of the publisher, except in the case of brief quotations embodied in critical reviews and certain other non-commercial uses permitted by copyright law.

© [2025] [Evelina J.G.]
All rights reserved.

PREFACE

Greetings from the Lyon Vacation Guide 2025, your all-in-one travel guide to one of France's most fascinating cities. Known as the world's culinary capital and a cultural gold mine, Lyon attracts tourists from all over the world with its unique mix of innovation, tradition, and charm.

This guide was painstakingly created to help you discover Lyon's greatest features, including its UNESCO World Heritage sites, lively districts, world-class museums, and busy marketplaces. This guide is intended to make your trip smooth, motivational, and memorable, regardless of whether you're lured by the prospect of enjoying Lyon's famous food, exploring the medieval alleyways of Vieux Lyon, or taking in the stunning contemporary architecture of La Confluence.

Practical advice, in-depth analyses of Lyon's rich history and culture, and carefully chosen itineraries for all types of travelers—from weekend adventurers to those looking for a weeklong adventure—can be found in the pages that follow. With advice on eco-friendly travel, family-friendly pursuits, and insider tips, this book guarantees that your vacation will be both meaningful and unforgettable.

Lyon continues to develop while remaining anchored in its extraordinary history as it gets ready to welcome tourists with open arms in 2025. Experience the distinct character of a city that skillfully combines the old and the modern with every walk along the Saône and Rhône riverfronts, every meal enjoyed in a classic bouchon, and all the hidden gems you'll find.

Whether you're visiting Lyon for the first time or again, we hope this guide will act as a guide and source of inspiration for your trip. As you explore the treasures of this remarkable city, may it bring you moments of pleasure, connection, and discovery.

Welcome to Lyon! The journey is just beginning!

TABLE OF CONTENTS

COPYRIGHT	2
PREFACE	3
TABLE OF CONTENTS	5
OVERVIEW	7
PLANNING YOUR TRIP	13
ACCOMMODATIONS	21
CULTURE AND HISTORY	29
CULINARY ADVENTURES	37
TOP ATTRACTIONS	45
ACTIVITIES AND EXPERIENCES	52
ANNUAL FESTIVALS AND EVENTS	59
SHOPPING	66
TIPS FOR FAMILIES	72
NIGHTLIFE	79
ECO-FRIENDLY TOURING	86
USEFUL REFERENCE	94
SAMPLE ITINERARIES	102
CONCLUDING REMARKS & SUGGESTIONS	110
CONTACTS AND RESOURCES	118

OVERVIEW

Reasons to Go to Lyon in 2025

Few cities in the world have the charm, history, and energy that combined to create a particular magnetism that invites visitors to experience something genuinely unique. In 2025, Lyon, the gastronomic capital of France, will provide all of that and more. Lyon offers a once-in-a-lifetime experience that satisfies the senses and uplifts the spirit, whether you're visiting for the first time or coming back to find hidden treasures.

Why come to Lyon this year? Because 2025 is a great year to visit a city that effortlessly combines the past and contemporary. Lyon's rich history, which includes Roman monuments and districts from the Renaissance, is woven into a dynamic current fabric that tells tales that date back centuries. However, Lyon's culture, cuisine, and friendly atmosphere are what really entice visitors to this vibrant city, not only its sites.

Lyon is positioned at the nexus of innovation and history in 2025. With cobblestone alleys, antique buildings, and secret tunnels just waiting to be discovered, Vieux Lyon, its charming old town, is recognized as a UNESCO World Heritage Site. This city, however, is known for its inventiveness in the fields of sustainability, technology, and the arts, and it is always changing. Lyon provides a singular chance to witness a city in action, brimming with vitality and excitement, whether you're strolling down the riverbank, indulging in a fine dining experience, or taking part in one of the numerous yearly events.

Synopsis of the History and Culture of Lyon

The history of Lyon is almost as fascinating as the city itself. Lyon, which is located where the Rhône and Saône rivers converge, has long been a hub for trade and culture. Lyon was the capital of the Roman province of Gallia Lugdunensis after being first established by the Romans in 43 BC as Lugdunum. From the old Fourvière amphitheater to the ruins of the Roman forum and baths that can be seen in the center of the city, this Roman influence is still felt across the whole city.

In the Middle Ages, Lyon developed into a significant hub for printing, textiles, and finance. Due to its position, the city had a significant part in forming France's cultural and economic landscapes and was a necessary stop along the European trade routes. Grand structures and magnificent palaces were built during this time, marking the beginning of Lyon's Renaissance. Many of these structures may still be seen in the Vieux Lyon neighborhood today.

Lyon became the center of France's silk industry in the 19th century, a legacy that continues to shape the city's character today. The boutiques that line the streets of the Croix-Rousse area, which was originally the center of the silk trade, are relics of this legacy. Lyon's strong ties to its industrial past are counterbalanced by its love of art, fashion, and cuisine, as you will discover when you visit the city.

Lyon is a city that embraces the future while honoring its varied heritage. With top-notch museums, a renowned opera theater, and innumerable galleries exhibiting both modern and classical art, its vibrant cultural landscape reflects this blending of the ancient and the new. The city attracts chefs, designers, and artists from all over the world, making it a center for creativity. Additionally, tradition is highly valued there, especially in its renowned food scene.

The "Lyonnais," or residents of Lyon, are extremely proud of their ancestry. They are hospitable and excited to introduce tourists to their city's rich culinary heritage and legendary past. With several Michelin-starred restaurants, traditional bouchons offering substantial Lyonnaise meals, and a thriving food market scene that includes the renowned Les Halles de Lyon, the city has earned its status as the gourmet capital of France. Lyon is a culinary lover's dream come true. Beyond the plate, however, Lyon is a city that promotes discovery and has a little bit of everything, from festivals and cultural events to green areas and walks along the river.

A Brief Overview of Lyon

One of the most fascinating places to visit in France is Lyon, a city rich in both modern elegance and historical strata. To help you get started on your trip, here are some brief facts:

In the southeast of France, in the Rhône-Alpes region, Lyon is situated approximately 470 kilometers (292 miles) southeast of Paris. The metropolitan region is home to more than 2 million people, while the city itself is home to about 520,000 people. The Fourvière Hill, Lyon's Old Town (Vieux Lyon), and its Traboules (secret tunnels) are all included in the UNESCO World Heritage Site.

- Cuisine: Known as France's culinary capital, Lyon is well-known for its culinary traditions and is home to well-known chefs like Paul Bocuse.

The Basilica of Notre-Dame de Fourvière, the Musée des Beaux-Arts, the Parc de la Tête d'Or, and the contemporary architecture of the Confluence neighborhood are all must-see sites.

- Language: English is generally understood in tourist areas, but French is the major language spoken.
- Transportation: The metro, buses, and trams are all excellent ways to get around Lyon. Lyon-Saint-Exupéry, the city's airport, serves both local and international travelers.
- Climate: Lyon is a fantastic destination all year round due to its moderate climate, which features scorching summers and pleasant winters.

Lyon observes daylight savings time (CEST) during the summer and runs on Central European Time (CET).

You'll quickly learn why Lyon is so adored by both inhabitants and tourists as soon as your journey begins. Its distinctive blend of culture, history, and fine dining creates an experience that is unlike any other and will linger in your memory long after you have left its quaint streets. Thus, prepare to discover Lyon in 2025—it will be ready to embrace you!

PLANNING YOUR TRIP

The Best Times to Go to Lyon

The time of day you choose to visit Lyon may have a significant impact on how you experience this amazing city. Whether you're attending festivals, going on outdoor excursions, or enjoying the city's renowned food, every season has its own appeal. The optimum time for your vacation will depend on what type of environment you'd want to enjoy.

From March to May, SPRING

Spring in Lyon is a very lovely time. The city comes alive with color as flowers blossom in parks and gardens, notably the breathtaking Parc de la Tête d'Or, and the temperature is pleasant. For those who enjoy taking walks by the river or exploring Lyon's lively outdoor cafés, spring is the ideal season. Because of the controlled crowds, you can take in the city's splendor without having to deal with the hustle and bustle of the busiest time of year. There are several exhibits and cultural events to check out this season if you're an art enthusiast.

June to August, SUMMER

Lyon experiences a pleasant and lively summer with temperatures between 25°C and 30°C (77°F and 86°F). Since this is the busiest time of year for tourists, the city will be teeming with activity, and there will be a lot of outdoor festivities to add to the excitement. Not to be missed is the yearly Nuits de Fourvière festival, which celebrates dance, theater, and music in the historic Roman theaters of Fourvière Hill in June and July. Enjoy a glass of local wine on a patio with a view of the Rhône on one of Lyon's charming summer evenings. The excitement of the season is definitely contagious, but be ready for increased costs and crowds.

September through November, FALL

Lyon is also a great place to come in the fall. The city is especially lovely as the leaves change color, casting a warm, golden glow over the city, and the summer crowds have subsided and the temperatures are still pleasant. The fall harvest season in neighboring Beaujolais is ideal for taking in Lyon's thriving wine culture. October is a season of expectation as the Festival of Lights (Fête des Lumières) begins to take shape. As the peak season comes to an end, you'll discover fantastic bargains on lodging, and the pleasant weather makes it ideal for walking or bicycling throughout the city.

December to February, WINTER
Lyon has a charming, enchanting atmosphere throughout the winter, particularly during the Festival of Lights (Fête des Lumières) in early December, when the city's landmarks and buildings are bathed in breathtaking light displays. Even though it may get cold, with lows of about 5°C (41°F), it's a great time to see Lyon's interior attractions, like its museums and restaurants. Because there are less tourists in the winter, you can get a more personal experience of the city, from exploring its sparkling streets to indulging in a hearty bowl of Lyonnaise soup at one of its renowned bouchons.

Directions to Lyon

Lyon's good transit connections make getting there simple. Lyon is well-served by a variety of transportation choices, whether you're coming in from overseas or going within France.

By Air:
The primary international entry point to the city is Lyon-Saint-Exupéry Airport (LYS), which is situated around 25 kilometers (15 miles) east of the city center. Travelers from all over the world find the airport handy since it has good connections to both international and major European locations. By tram, taxi, or private transfer, you may quickly get to the city center once you're there. The tram travel takes around 30 minutes, whereas a cab ride will take roughly 40 minutes.

By Train: Lyon is well-connected by train, and Gare Part-Dieu is the city's central train station, offering high-speed TGV connections to Paris, Marseille, and other important cities. For those departing from the French capital, the train is a rapid and practical choice, taking around two hours to get to Lyon. With beautiful routes through the French countryside, the train is also a great choice if you're traveling from other European towns like Geneva or Milan.

By Automobile:
Renting a car might be a fantastic choice if you intend to explore the nearby areas. Lyon's location at the crossroads of several highways,

including the A6 and A7, makes it conveniently accessible by vehicle. You may visit the charming medieval village of Pérouges or the neighboring vineyards of Beaujolais if you choose to drive to Lyon. However, be advised that parking in the city center can be difficult and costly, and that traffic can get backed up, particularly during rush hour.

Lyon Transportation

Lyon's first-rate public transit system makes traveling throughout the city easy and pleasurable. Lyon's transportation choices make it simple to get around, whether your plans involve seeing the city's historic monuments, dining at its well-known restaurants, or shopping at its stylish shops.

Public Transportation: TCL (Transports en Commun Lyonnais) is in charge of Lyon's extensive and effective public transportation system. All of the city's main neighborhoods and attractions are connected by buses, four metro lines, and many tram lines. The Lyon City Card is a great option for travelers because it provides unrestricted access to all public transportation, including the funicular to Fourvière Hill. The trams are a convenient way to see the city at your own speed, and the metro operates frequently from early in the morning until about midnight.

Scooters and bicycles:
You may hire bikes or electric scooters through a number of programs, such as the city's bike-sharing program Vélo'v, for a more active and environmentally responsible mode of transportation. The picturesque banks of the Rhône and Saône are especially enjoyable for riding, and Lyon is a bike-friendly city.

Ride-sharing and taxis:
Although they might cost extra, taxis are widely accessible around the city. In Lyon, ride-sharing services like Uber are also available, providing a practical and occasionally less expensive option to conventional taxis.

Setting a Travel Budget

Whether you're searching for an inexpensive vacation or an opulent stay, Lyon has a lot to offer to fit any budget. Below is a summary of what to anticipate:

Lodging:
From opulent five-star hotels in the Presqu'île neighborhood to quaint boutique hotels in Vieux Lyon, Lyon offers a wide variety of lodging options. A mid-range hotel room will cost around €100 to €300 per night, while hostels and guesthouses are more affordable, with rates ranging from €50 to €80 per night. Consider renting an apartment for a cozier atmosphere if you want a more distinctive experience.

Dining and Meals:
Lyon is known for its cuisine, and there are many affordable dining options available. While casual restaurants and cafés serve food for about €10 to €15, a traditional bouchon will set you back between €20 and €40 for a meal. A full-course meal at a Michelin-starred restaurant or gourmet dining establishment will cost at least €100 per person. Street food, including local pastries and crepes, is a terrific budget-friendly alternative, often costing €5–€10.

institutions and Activities: Most museums and cultural institutions charge between €5 and €15 for admission, which is often reasonable. At about €30 for two days, the

Lyon City Card is a terrific deal, including free admission to several institutions and unrestricted public transportation. Lyon is a great city to see without going over budget because of its free attractions, which include strolling around the historic districts and the city's lovely parks.

You can enjoy all that Lyon has to offer, whether you're dining in style, taking in the city's cultural treasures, or just taking in the ambience in one of its charming squares, if you plan ahead and keep your spending in check.

ACCOMMODATIONS

From opulent hotels with first-rate amenities to quaint guesthouses and affordable hostels, Lyon has a variety of lodging choices to fit every taste and budget. There is the ideal spot to unwind after a day of touring, regardless of how long you want to remain in the city.

Options for Lodging

There are many different lodging options in Lyon, and each one offers something special to meet the demands of various tourists. Here is a summary of your possibilities, regardless of whether you're looking for comfort or indulgence:

Exotic Accommodations

There are many upscale hotels in Lyon if you want to spoil yourself with a lavish stay. Your vacation will be genuinely unforgettable because of these places' first-rate amenities, stunning vistas, and flawless service.

A notable choice is the five-star Villa Maia hotel, which is tucked away on Fourvière Hill.

This hotel, which offers breathtaking city views, is ideal for those seeking a tranquil getaway since it blends contemporary grandeur with understated elegance. Gourmet cuisine, a full-service spa, and a warm, inviting setting make guests feel pampered from beginning to end. The magnificent Renaissance-style hotel Cour des Loges, located in the center of Vieux Lyon, is another great option. Its opulent suites provide first-rate facilities and a sense of Lyon's rich past, replete with historical décor and contemporary conveniences.

The InterContinental Lyon - Hôtel-Dieu is a magnificent choice for anyone seeking to combine luxury with first-rate service. This hotel, which is housed in a beautifully renovated historic structure, has luxurious suites, a gorgeous glass-domed atrium, and a number of excellent dining options. A stay at one of these opulent hotels will enhance your experience if you're in Lyon for a special event.

Stays in the Midrange

Lyon offers a large selection of reasonably priced hotels that are ideal for those seeking comfort without going over budget. These lodgings guarantee that you may enjoy everything the city has to offer without going over budget by combining first-rate service, comfortable rooms, and prime locations.

A fantastic mid-range choice is the Hotel Silky by HappyCulture, which is conveniently located in Lyon's bustling dining and retail districts. The chic, contemporary rooms provide a tranquil setting, and complimentary tea and coffee are provided to visitors, personalizing their stay. Another excellent alternative is the Mercure Lyon Centre Beaux-Arts, which is well located in the Presqu'île neighborhood and provides a chic yet reasonably priced choice for visitors looking to see the city's cultural center. It is a favorite with tourists who like to be near all the excitement because of its excellent location and contemporary facilities.

The Lyon Marriott Hotel Cité Internationale has large rooms and a warm ambiance for people looking for a little more homely. It's conveniently adjacent to cultural sites and the Parc de la Tête d'Or, making it a great starting point for exploring Lyon's lovely green areas while remaining close to the vibrant city center.

Inexpensive Guesthouses and Hostels

Lyon has a range of reasonably priced and cozy hostels and guesthouses for those on a restricted budget. These choices offer a more sociable experience, frequently with common areas and a laid-back ambiance, making them perfect for young tourists or those looking for a more lively setting.

One of Lyon's best hostels, SLO Living Hostel, is located in the Confluence neighborhood of the city and offers private rooms and contemporary, chic dormitories. In addition to having a café, this social and environmentally conscious hostel is a terrific place to meet other tourists. Another inexpensive find in the center of the city is the Ho36 Hostel. This hostel is ideal for individuals seeking comfort and cost because it offers both private rooms and dorm beds, as well as comfortable facilities and a relaxed atmosphere.

Consider booking a room in a guesthouse in the charming Old Town, like La Maison de la Tour, for a more private experience. This guesthouse provides a cozy substitute for the typical hotel with its historic charm and friendly ambience. It's the perfect starting point for discovering Lyon at your own leisure because of the personal touches and the breathtaking beauty of the city.

Best Places to Reside

Every district in Lyon has something special to offer when it comes to lodging. Whether you're interested in Confluence's contemporary ambiance or Vieux Lyon's heritage, each location offers a unique environment that can improve your trip. The following is a list of some of Lyon's top neighborhoods:

Vieux Lyon

One of Lyon's most quaint and ancient districts is Vieux Lyon, often known as Old Town. Vieux Lyon, a UNESCO World Heritage Site, is a tangle of Renaissance structures, cobblestone lanes, and secret tunnels called traboules. With breathtaking views of the Basilique Notre-Dame de Fourvière and convenient access to some of Lyon's most famous sights, staying here will allow you to fully immerse yourself in the city's rich history.

A variety of boutique hotels, quaint guesthouses, and antique homes can be found in Vieux Lyon. The neighborhood's lively cafés and bouchons, as well as its close proximity to local attractions, make it a great choice for first-time tourists, regardless of whether they opt for a luxurious hotel or a comfortable bed & breakfast.

Presqu'île

The city's business and cultural center is the Presqu'île neighborhood, which is situated between the Rhône and Saône rivers. Wide boulevards, high-end stores, art galleries, and museums, such as the Museum of Fine Arts of Lyon (Musée des Beaux-Arts), are all present in this neighborhood. For people who love the bustle of the city and want to live near Lyon's vibrant cultural scene, this is the ideal location.

For those looking for a more autonomous stay, the Presqu'île offers a number of mid-range and expensive hotels in addition to apartment rentals. Additionally, the neighborhood is dotted with lively cafés, modern eateries, and cocktail bars. Presqu'île provides a vibrant and elegant setting for your visit if you like to be in the middle of everything.

Rousse Croix

Known for its distinctive fusion of bohemian appeal and historical relevance, Croix-Rousse is a hilltop district located on the city's northern edge. With unique boutiques, art galleries, and welcoming cafés dotting the sidewalks, this area—once the center of Lyon's silk industry—has a strong creative influence. During your visit, you may also explore the Traboules de la Croix-Rousse in the vicinity.

There are a variety of affordable lodging alternatives, quaint guesthouses, and boutique hotels in the area. Away from the bustling tourist crowds, staying here offers a more relaxed, local experience where you can take in Lyon's creative vitality.

Confluence

Visit the Confluence district, which has seen significant construction recently, for a more modern feel. Confluence is a fantastic spot to stay for individuals seeking a more contemporary, urban experience because of its modern architecture, chic shopping centers, and riverfront vistas. Numerous eco-friendly hotels and lodging options with a focus on design can also be found there.

Confluence is conveniently located near the recently constructed Musée des Confluences, a beautiful science and anthropology museum housed in a futuristic structure, and has good access to the rest of Lyon. Confluence is a great option for tourists interested in contemporary design and culture because of its hip stores, creative restaurants, and vibrant environment.

CULTURE AND HISTORY

The city of Lyon has changed over the ages, fusing its dynamic modernity with its historical heritage. Every area of this stunning city has a tale to tell, from the Roman to the Renaissance and beyond. From its period as a major Roman colony to its importance as a hub for the silk trade to its current status as a center for modern architecture and innovation, discovering Lyon's history and culture is a voyage through time. A closer look into Lyon's intriguing history may be found here.

World Heritage Sites by UNESCO

Lyon has a distinguished place on the UNESCO World Heritage list because of its rich history and cultural significance. The city's two primary heritage districts, Vieux Lyon and The Presqu'île, provide witness to its transformation from the medieval and Renaissance eras to the vibrant, contemporary metropolis it is today.

The city's Old Town, Vieux Lyon, with its cobblestone streets and exquisitely maintained Renaissance structures, is an outdoor museum.

The city's intriguing past may be revealed by exploring its winding streets and finding secret courtyards and stairs. It's like entering a living history book as you stroll through this neighborhood, where quaint squares and cathedrals like Saint-Jean Cathedral provide hints about the city's medieval past.

Situated between the Rhône and Saône rivers, the Presqu'île is another UNESCO-listed region that perfectly captures the architectural and historical significance of Lyon. It is a terrific spot to study the city's more recent past because of its magnificent avenues and squares, which are dotted with classical structures and excellent examples of 19th-century urban design. This neighborhood exemplifies Lyon's ability to strike a balance between the past and the present with its blend of neoclassical architecture and a thriving cultural environment.

In addition to offering an aesthetic experience, seeing these UNESCO World Heritage Sites enables you to comprehend the city's crucial role in European history.

Ancient Theaters and Sites in Roman Lyon

Lyon's history dates back to the Roman era, when it was the capital of Roman Gaul and was known as Lugdunum. Located all across Lyon, the city's historic Roman sites provide a fascinating look into Roman culture.

An enormous outdoor theater that dates back to the first century BC, the Ancient Theatre of Fourvière is one of Lyon's most impressive Roman ruins. In keeping with its long history, the theater, which formerly had space for more than 10,000 people, continues to host performances during the Nuits de Fourvière festival. With expansive city vistas as a breathtaking background, you can see the magnificent performances that once delighted the people of Lugdunum while you're standing in the theater.

You may learn more about the history and relics of the Roman era at the Gallo-Roman Museum of Lyon-Fourvière, which is only a short stroll from the theater. Ancient sculptures, mosaics, and commonplace items from the museum's collection offer visitors a physical link to the local population from thousands of years ago. Another Roman ruin worth seeing is the Temple of Cybele, which is located just behind the museum and displays the city's formerly thriving religious life.

Knowing how Lyon developed into a crucial hub of trade, politics, and culture in antiquity is essential to appreciating its Roman legacy. You are entering the past when you walk through these historic locations, surrounded by the ruins of a civilization that had a significant influence on the city.

Vieux Lyon Renaissance Charm

You will be taken back to the Renaissance era as you explore Vieux Lyon, when the city was a thriving hub for banking, trade, and culture. The area is a living reminder of Lyon's 16th-century splendor, with its meandering cobblestone lanes, pastel-colored houses, and elaborate façades.

Vieux Lyon's architecture is a stunning blend of medieval and Renaissance design, with graceful traboules—secret tunnels connecting buildings and courtyards—providing an insight into the daily routines of the city's past residents. Because they allowed the silk weavers who worked in Lyon's booming textile industry to carry their wares without being exposed to the weather, these traboules were particularly crucial.

The Saint-Jean Cathedral, a magnificent example of Gothic architecture with elaborate stained glass windows and an amazing astronomical clock, is one of the district's most famous features. During the Renaissance, Lyon's ecclesiastical and cultural prominence was symbolized by the cathedral.

Visit the Maison des Canuts to discover more about Lyon's famed silk-weaving heritage. During the Renaissance, one of the city's most important exports was silk, and a visit to this museum offers an intriguing look into the artistry that made Lyon renowned across Europe. The artisan stores of Vieux Lyon still showcase the delicate elegance of Lyon's silk scarves and textiles, giving this area of the city a timeless aura.

The vibrant ambiance of Vieux Lyon, where cafes overflow onto the streets and conversation and laughter abound, adds to the city's Renaissance appeal. It's simple to see yourself as a part of the rich tapestry of history that took place here as you stroll through the winding lanes.

La Confluence's Modern Architecture

Lyon has a rich history, but its future is as fascinating. Situated at the southernmost point of the Presqu'île, the Confluence, the neighborhood is a shining example of contemporary architectural innovation and urban revitalization. Sleek modern structures and sustainable urban planning have been combined to create a state-of-the-art center of current design in this formerly industrial neighborhood.

The Musée des Confluences, a remarkable science and anthropology museum set in a futuristic glass-and-steel edifice, is one of Confluence's most notable attractions. Although its distinctive shape—that of a spacecraft or a crystal—stands in stark contrast to Lyon's more conventional architecture, it blends in perfectly with the district's forward-thinking philosophy. The museum is a must-visit for anybody interested in learning as much about the future as the past because of its thought-provoking displays on science, human history, and the natural world.

A variety of contemporary residences, retail establishments, and office buildings that were all created with sustainability in mind can also be found in the Confluence neighborhood. It demonstrates Lyon's ability to embrace the future while preserving a strong regard for its history. Lyon seems to be both looking back and moving forward because of the dynamic energy created by the contrast between its modern and ancient areas.

You can see the creative, sustainable, and inventive character of contemporary Lyon by strolling through the Confluence neighborhood. It provides an idea of what Lyon will look like in the future by bringing together modern living with the city's rich past.

Every street, structure, and neighborhood of Lyon is infused with its history and culture, providing a vibrant fusion of the ancient, the Renaissance, and the contemporary. Lyon welcomes you to explore its history, present, and future, whether you're gazing at the ruins of Roman theaters, taking in Vieux Lyon's Renaissance architecture, or discovering Confluence's modernism. The rich cultural tapestry that makes Lyon such a distinctive destination to visit is enhanced by each of these distinct layers.

CULINARY ADVENTURES

With good reason, Lyon is frequently referred to as France's culinary capital. With each dish telling a tale, each ingredient having a backstory, and each mouthful leaving an impression on your senses, the city has a rich culinary culture that extends beyond the plate. If you have a passion for cuisine, you just must visit Lyon. Lyon provides a veritable feast for the senses, with its inventive modern cuisine and rich culinary legacy. Every area of the city offers something special and remarkable.

Overview of Lyonnaise Food

Hearty, rustic tastes and a love of fresh, local ingredients are hallmarks of Lyonnaise cuisine. The topography of the area has a big impact on Lyon's food; the city's closeness to the Rhône and Saône rivers, as well as the lush countryside that surrounds it, provide an abundance of fresh meat, seafood, and vegetables. The city's culinary origins may be found in its working-class past, when inexpensive ingredients were used to make straightforward, tasty meals. Although this cuisine has developed and become more sophisticated over time, its emphasis on flavor depth and richness has never changed.

The famous bouchons, historic restaurants where you may try the best of the city's gastronomic offerings, are at the center of Lyonnaise cuisine. Lyon's passion for food is rooted in history, culture, and the unifying power of food, not only in its flavor. The city's chefs are known for their painstaking attention to detail, frequently transforming ordinary materials into remarkable meals. Lyon provides a genuine culinary experience unlike any other, whether you're enjoying a dainty pastry or a hearty platter of quenelles.

Recipes You Must Try

Every dish in the exquisite variety of Lyonnaise cuisine is more delicious than the one before it. If you're planning a gastronomic trip in Lyon, there are a few delicacies you absolutely must miss.

One highlight is Quenelles de Brochet, a trademark Lyonnaise meal prepared from pike fish that is poached and served in a rich, creamy sauce. The quenelles have a soft, decadent texture and are delicate but gratifying. It's the ideal way to start exploring Lyon's diverse culinary culture, especially when paired with a glass of the region's white wine.

Salade Lyonnaise, a traditional appetizer consisting of crispy bacon, fresh frisée lettuce, a poached egg, and a zesty mustard vinaigrette, is another must-try. Its flawless harmony of tastes and textures is a real example of Lyon's talent for bringing out the best in basic ingredients.

Try Tête de Veau, a meal of soft veal's head served with a delicious ravigote sauce, for a more decadent experience. Despite its peculiar sound, this is a well-liked Lyonnaise dish that exemplifies the city's custom of utilizing every part of the animal to produce mouthwatering, nuanced tastes.

Lyon is renowned for its charcuterie as well. Another classic is the pork sausage known as andouillette. It pairs best with a glass of Beaujolais or Côtes du Rhône wine, both of which are produced in the area, to complement its unique rich, smokey flavor.

Examining Bouchons: Classic Lyon Dining Establishments

No visit to Lyon would be complete without dining at a traditional bouchon. These intimate, often family-run restaurants are the heart and soul of Lyonnaise cuisine. With wooden furniture, gingham tablecloths, and a rustic charm that transports one back in time, the ambiance is cozy and inviting.

The food at a bouchon is usually straightforward but incredibly filling. The greatest of Lyonnaise cuisine may be found in the form of filling stews, succulent meats, and cozy sides. One of the city's most well-known bouchons, Le Café des Fédérations, is renowned for its authentic Lyonnaise cuisine and friendly ambiance. Simmer the Pot-au-feu to perfection, a rich beef stew served with vegetables.

A more modern spin on the traditional bouchon may be found at Les Lyonnais, a chic and contemporary Lyonnaise restaurant that nonetheless serves all the region's favorite dishes with a few inventive twists.

The experience of dining at a bouchon is just as important as the cuisine. The wine flows as readily as the discussions, and the servers are frequently like old friends. The authentic essence of Lyon's culinary culture is embodied in these locations.

The Legacy of Paul Bocuse

No debate about Lyon's culinary culture is complete without discussing Paul Bocuse, the great chef who helped place the city on the world gourmet map. Bocuse's effect on Lyonnaise cuisine cannot be emphasized. His restaurant, L'Auberge du Pont de Collonges, just outside the city, has received three Michelin stars for decades and is a hallmark of French culinary excellence.

Bocuse was noted for his inventive approach to traditional French cuisine, mixing old techniques with modern flare. He believed in using fresh, local ingredients and elevating them to new heights. His signature dish, Soupe aux Truffes V.G.E., a sumptuous truffle soup served in a puff pastry dome, is a wonderful illustration of his culinary talent.

Bocuse's impact endures in Lyon's culinary scene, motivating next generations of chefs and continuing to shape the global perception of Lyonnaise cuisine. The Musée Paul Bocuse, dedicated to his life and work, is a must-visit for food lovers, offering a deep dive into his culinary philosophy and a look at his iconic dishes.

Food Markets: Les Halles de Lyon and More

Visit one of the well-known food markets in Lyon for a genuinely immersive gastronomic experience. Les Halles de Lyon Paul Bocuse is the most renowned, a bustling indoor market that is a food lover's paradise. All of Lyon's finest cheeses, charcuterie, fresh produce, and pastries are available here. Locals buy there for the ingredients they use every day, while tourists may sample the local cuisine.

The market is named after Paul Bocuse, and it's easy to understand why—it's a celebration of the finest regional goods. Explore the stalls, try some of the cheeses, have a piece of salami, and don't forget to get a few freshly made brioche to go with you.

For a more local experience, consider visiting the Marché de la Croix-Rousse, a charming outdoor market that takes place in the lively Croix-Rousse district. Fresh fruits and veggies, organic meats, and homemade jams are just a few of the artisanal goods available here.

Regional Wines and Drinks

No supper in Lyon would be complete without the proper wine to complement it. The area is renowned for its superb wines, and every gastronomic journey must include a stop at a local cave (wine cellar).

The region's most well-known wine, Beaujolais, is renowned for its fruity, light flavor. The wine, made from the Gamay grapes go well with Lyon's rich cuisine, especially the charcuterie. A Côtes du Rhône wine, which is usually a combination of Grenache, Syrah, and Mourvèdre grapes, offers a deeper, spicier taste if you're searching for something a bit more powerful.

Apart from wine, Lyon is known for its distinctive drinks, such Cerdon, a rosé that sparkles just enough to be enjoyed on a bright afternoon. And don't forget to taste a glass of Quintaine—a pleasant, fruit-based liqueur that's particularly popular in the summer months.

Lyon's gastronomic journey appeals to all senses. Long after you go, the rich flavors, vivid colors, and aromatic scents will continue to weave a tapestry of flavors in your mind. Whether you're tasting a typical bouchon meal, learning the heritage of Paul Bocuse, or visiting the busy food markets, Lyon guarantees a delightful adventure you'll never forget.

TOP ATTRACTIONS

Adventure awaits you everywhere in Lyon, a city rich in culture, history, and scenic beauty. There are plenty of thrilling adventures just waiting to be found, ranging from breathtaking vistas and architectural wonders to tranquil parks and little secret passageways. Lyon has something unique to offer everyone, whether they are history buffs, art lovers, or nature lovers. Let's explore the main draws that will make this city an essential travel destination in 2025.

Notre-Dame de Fourvière Basilica

The Basilica of Notre-Dame de Fourvière is a magnificent site that dominates the Lyon skyline, perched high on the hill of Fourvière. Constructed in the late 19th century, this spectacular church offers an adventure in addition to a spiritual experience. Ascending to the basilica offers sweeping views of the city, including Lyon's picturesque rooftops, meandering rivers, and far-off mountains.

The basilica's interior is equally breathtaking. The interior's elaborate mosaics, gilded accents, and tall stained-glass windows gleam. With a figure of the Virgin Mary that has come to represent the city's protection, the Chapel of the Virgin is a highlight. Before seeing the basilica's magnificent interiors, if you're feeling really daring, ride the Funicular up to the mountaintop, which is an entertaining and picturesque way to get there. For anyone seeking an even more breathtaking viewpoint, the panoramic terrace provides one of Lyon's greatest views, ideal for taking memorable pictures.

The Tête d'Or Park

Visit Lyon's largest and most well-known park, Parc de la Tête d'Or, for a revitalizing getaway into nature. This beautiful, spacious green park comprises 290 acres, providing visitors the right balance of calm and excitement. This park is a haven in the middle of the city, whether you want to explore the botanical gardens, take a boat ride, or just take a leisurely stroll around the tranquil lake.

Families will enjoy the park's zoo, which features a range of animals, such as giraffes, lions, and monkeys, all surrounded by lovely gardens. The zoo is a great place for a leisurely day out because admission is free. With themed gardens like the tropical greenhouse and the rose garden, the botanical garden is a botanical paradise for people who enjoy plants from all over the world. You might easily spend a whole day here, having a picnic by the lake or just relaxing in the shade of the park and taking in the tranquil surroundings.

The Museum of Fine Arts

Musée des Beaux-Arts is a must-see if culture and the arts are your top priorities. With a vast collection spanning centuries of creative history, this world-class museum—one of France's greatest fine arts museums—is housed in a former convent. In addition to an intriguing collection of sculptures, antiques, and even modern art, you'll discover pieces by some of the greatest masters, such as Rembrandt, Goya, and Monet.

The museum is divided into parts, each of which provides a unique experience. The Italian Renaissance gallery is a highlight, showcasing exquisite paintings from artists such as Titian and Raphael. The 19th-century gallery offers more recent pieces that evoke the mood of the time, such as Delacroix and

Renoir. After perusing the museum's extensive collection, spend some time unwinding in the garden, a tranquil area ideal for contemplating the artwork you have viewed.

Confluences Museum

Make sure to visit the Musée des Confluences for an entirely new viewpoint on Lyon's past and future. Located at the junction of the Rhône and Saône rivers, this stunningly futuristic museum is as much about its architecture as it is about its displays. The structure itself, meant to seem like a spacecraft, is a visual wonder, with sharp angles and glass panels that reflect the surrounding scenery.

Inside, the museum is as intriguing. Its natural history, anthropology, and science displays provide an engaging and immersive experience. The permanent collections span everything from ancient civilizations to space exploration, giving a fascinating journey through human history and the natural world. The fossil collection, which transports you back millions of years to a time when life on Earth was quite different, is one of the most notable aspects. Awe and curiosity will be sparked in everyone who visits the museum because of its design and its thought-provoking exhibits.

Traboules: Lyon's Secret Routes

Lyon is a city of secrets, with secret courtyards, narrow streets, and quaint lanes that evoke the past. The traboules, hidden passageways that wind through the center of the city, are among the most intriguing of these. Silk workers used to move their wares via these slender, covered passageways to avoid the weather. They now provide a distinctive means of city exploration, providing insights into Lyon's obscure past.

Visit La Croix-Rousse or Vieux Lyon to enjoy the traboules. Keep an eye out for the doorways leading to the traboules as you navigate the Old Town's winding streets. Be considerate if you enter these passageways, as some are accessible to the general public and others are concealed behind private homes. The traboules are small, personal, and rich in history; it's like traveling back in time. A memorable aspect of Lyon's allure, many of the traboules are embellished with lovely courtyards and ornamental architecture.

The Riverfronts of the Saône and Rhône

Exploring Lyon's breathtaking riverfronts is one of the finest ways to get a sense of the city's spirit. The city is situated between the Rhône and Saône rivers, each of which provides a unique yet equally stunning view of the city. The riverfronts are a great place to admire Lyon's splendor, whether you're taking a leisurely stroll, going on a boat trip, or just relaxing by the water's edge.

The Saône riverfront, with its quaint quays and cobblestone streets, is especially picturesque. There are comfortable cafes and eateries here where you can sit and observe the passing boats or go on a picturesque boat ride to get a water view of Lyon. The riverfront of the Rhône is dotted with contemporary structures, parks, and open areas, making it the perfect spot to unwind or go for a bike ride. If you're feeling more adventurous, consider hiring a kayak or stand-up paddleboard to explore the rivers at your own leisure.

Both rivers provide a different slice of Lyon's ambiance, whether it's the ancient, intimate vibe along the Saône or the vibrant, contemporary energy along the Rhône. Not only are the riverfronts picturesque, but they also play a crucial role in Lyon's identity by intriguingly tying the city's past and present together.

From ancient history to modern innovation, from natural beauty to undiscovered secrets, Lyon's top attractions provide a plethora of experiences. Whether you're exploring the grandeur of Notre-Dame de Fourvière, meandering through the serene beauty of Parc de la Tête d'Or, or finding the hidden gems in the city's traboules, there's no shortage of adventure in this dynamic city. Every location narrates a tale, resulting in a journey through one of France's most vibrant and captivating cities that will never be forgotten.

ACTIVITIES AND EXPERIENCES

Lyon is a place to experience rather than merely visit. There are several opportunities for adventure, from bicycling along its riverfronts to taking a leisurely stroll through its ancient neighborhoods. Lyon has a range of activities that will keep you interested, energized, and engrossed in the city's charm, regardless of your interests—whether you're an outdoor enthusiast, history buff, or someone searching for a novel approach to explore. Prepare to explore Lyon from every perspective as you set out on life-changing adventures that will make the city come to life.

Tours for Biking and Walking

Walking or riding a bike are two of the greatest ways to see Lyon. The city is a great place for walking tours that highlight its rich history and hidden treasures because of its small size and pedestrian-friendly streets. A walking tour provides an intimate and personal experience of the city's layers, whether you're exploring the mysteries of its traboules or meandering through the cobblestone streets of Vieux Lyon.

Bike tours are an excellent opportunity for outdoor enthusiasts to experience Lyon from a new angle and to step up their exploration. It's simple to get on a bike and explore the city's many varied districts thanks to its vast network of bike routes and Vélo'v bike-sharing stations. One of the most fun bike paths follows the Rhône and Saône rivers, where you can glide by new buildings and ancient sites while taking in breathtaking views of the city skyline. To give you a sense of Lyon's lively, everyday life, many trips also include stops to lesser-known locations that only locals are aware of, such as local markets.

Consider taking a guided walking tour of Lyon's UNESCO-listed Old Town if you're interested in history. There, you'll learn about the city's intriguing past, which includes its Roman origins, Renaissance impact, and silk-weaving background. Or take a Gastronomic Walking Tour to experience Lyon's cuisine while exploring its most well-known food markets, cafés, and bouchons. A hands-on, knowledgeable-led walking tour is the best way to discover the city's unique culinary culture.

Boat Rides and River Cruises

One of the most memorable ways to explore the attractions is to take a boat along the banks of Lyon's two rivers, the Rhône and the Saône, which create an enchanted background for the city. You may find a boat experience for everyone, whether you're looking for a vibrant sightseeing cruise or a leisurely sunset trip.

Climb aboard a traditional bateau lyonnais for a more private and picturesque experience. These quaint wooden boats provide sweeping views of Lyon's old buildings and bridges as they float over the Saône. The magnificent Basilica of Notre-Dame de Fourvière atop its hill, the graceful riverbank promenades, and the unique architecture of the Presqu'île neighborhood will all be seen from a new angle as you sail through the center of the city. Numerous trips are guided by experienced tour guides who will impart intriguing facts about Lyon's past and how the city has been shaped by the rivers.

Try a stand-up paddleboard or kayak trip on the Rhône if you're feeling very daring. Paddling along the river's side is a great way to see Lyon's lively environment because of the serene waters and stunning sights. Consider a dinner cruise for a more opulent experience, where you may have a delectable meal while taking in the breathtaking city views at night.

Lyon Day Trips

Although Lyon offers a wealth of activities, its central location in the Rhône-Alpes region makes it an ideal starting point for some amazing day excursions. There is a lot to discover only a short drive from the city, including world-class wine areas, ancient towns, and the magnificent French Alps.

Wine Region of Beaujolais

A visit to the Beaujolais Wine Region is a must-do for every wine enthusiast. This gorgeous area, which is only 30 minutes north of Lyon, is well-known for its vineyards, undulating hills, and quaint villages. The Gamay grape, which is the most well-known product of Beaujolais, yields fruity, light wines that are ideal for enjoying while taking in the breathtaking scenery.

You may discover Beaujolais by taking a wine tour, which will show you around the vineyards and give you the opportunity to taste some of the greatest wines the area has to offer while also teaching you about the winemaking process. Numerous excursions also include a stop to a local wine cellar, where you may sample the wines directly from the barrel and learn about the age-old methods that contribute to the distinctiveness of Beaujolais wines. A delightful lunch at a local vineyard, where you can savor regional specialties like charcuterie, cheeses, and freshly baked bread while admiring the vines, is a great way to complement your wine tasting for a more immersive experience.

Medieval Village Pérouges

Visit Pérouges, one of France's most exquisite medieval villages, for a glimpse into the past. About 35 kilometers northeast of Lyon, this little town appears to be stuck in time thanks to its cobblestone streets, strong walls, and well-preserved medieval homes. You'll think you've stepped into a fairy tale as you meander through the winding passageways.

Pérouges has a rich history in addition to its natural beauty. Many of the homes have elaborate architectural characteristics, and the community was formerly a thriving hub for silk production. As you tour the ancient alleyways, don't forget to stop by one of the neighborhood cafés for a sample of the village's well-known galette de Pérouges, a sweet, buttery pastry that's the ideal treat. Pérouges provides an engaging day trip, whether you're exploring the village's history or taking photographs of the lovely surroundings.

The French Alps and Annecy

The town of Annecy, which is located at the base of the French Alps, is a bit further away, but well worth the trip. Annecy, sometimes referred to as the "Venice of the Alps" because of its attractive old town and picturesque canals, is a place that combines historical appeal with natural splendor. From Lyon, it's only a two-hour journey, making it a simple yet thrilling day excursion.

One of the most beautiful lakes in Europe, the Lac d'Annecy, is the main attraction of Annecy. If you're feeling more daring, try stand-up paddleboarding or kayaking, or take a leisurely boat trip on the lake. With hiking and bike routes that give expansive views of the lake and valley below, the neighboring mountains make for a striking background. Explore the old town's cobblestone lanes, where quaint shops and cafés beckon and colorful buildings border the canals. A memorable day excursion from Lyon is to Annecy, where leisure and adventure collide.

Lyon is a city that encourages exploration, both inside its boundaries and in the breathtaking surroundings. The experiences that lie ahead are as varied as they are thrilling, whether you're taking in the alpine splendor of Annecy, sampling regional wines in Beaujolais, or traveling back in time in Pérouges. So put on your walking shoes, go on a bike, or set sail along the rivers—you're going to have an incredible time that will make your trip to Lyon one to remember.

ANNUAL FESTIVALS AND EVENTS

With festivals and events honoring art, culture, history, and the changing of the seasons, Lyon is a city that comes alive with vitality, inventiveness, and color all year long. Lyon's yearly events cater to all tastes, whether you're an art fan, music lover, or just someone who enjoys seeing a city at its liveliest. Festivals in the city are a reflection of its modern, inventive attitude as well as its rich cultural legacy. Here are a few of the most amazing occasions that make Lyon a year-round visit to remember.

The Festival of Lights, or Fête des Lumières

The Fête des Lumières, or Festival of Lights, is one of Lyon's most famous celebrations, turning the city into a breathtaking display each December. Since its inception in 1852, this cherished custom has grown to become one of the biggest light festivals globally. Lyon is transformed into a living canvas of color and innovation for four enchanted evenings when its streets, squares, and landmarks are bathed in dazzling light displays.

Beginning as an homage to Saint Barbara, when Lyon inhabitants lit candles in their windows to honor the Virgin Mary, the event celebrated the city's history and relationship to light. With light works and projections created by artists from all over the world, the event has already expanded into a huge worldwide attraction. Visitors can explore captivating light sculptures, interactive exhibits, and installations that narrate tales of wonder and imagination at some of the festival's most famous sites, including the Basilica of Notre-Dame de Fourvière, Place Bellecour, and the banks of the Saône River.

The Fête des Lumières offers an opportunity to see the city in a whole new way, both physically and figuratively, in addition to being a visual experience. This festival unites both locals and visitors, fostering a sense of wonder and festivity that lights up Lyon's streets. This event is a must-see, regardless of whether you're going for the first time or coming back to take in the light displays.

Festival of Nuits Sonores Music

One of the most significant electronic music festivals in Europe, the Nuits Sonores Music Festival, puts Lyon's thriving music scene front and center. With concerts that last far into the morning, Nuits Sonores, which takes place every spring, turns the city into a refuge for underground music. The event draws both well-known performers and up-and-coming musicians because of its diverse selection of electronic genres, which range from house and techno to experimental and indie sounds.

The way that Nuits Sonores incorporates Lyon's urban areas into its festival experience is what really sets it apart. Venues ranging from subterranean clubs and industrial warehouses to outdoor stages and historic structures host concerts and DJ performances across the city. The festival's distinctive fusion of local and international performers, as well as its immersive utilization of Lyon's streets and spaces, generates an electrifying environment that appeals to both adventure seekers and music enthusiasts.

Beyond the shows, Nuits Sonores serves as a forum for artistic exchanges, debates, and seminars that delve into the nexus of technology, art, and music. Attending seminars, seeing sound installations, and learning more about the changing music industry are all options for individuals who wish to delve deeper into the realm of electronic music. Nuits Sonores is more than simply a festival; it's a chance to see Lyon from the perspective of innovative music and artistic expression.

The Dance Biennale

Another important occasion that demonstrates Lyon's strong ties to the arts is the Biennale de la Danse. This festival, which celebrates dance in all its forms—from modern and classical to urban and traditional styles—occurs every two years in September. Some of the most famous dancers, choreographers, and companies in the world perform in Lyon's theaters, streets, and public areas over the period of several weeks.

The city's varied cultural scene is explored via a variety of performances, workshops, and activities during the Biennale de la Danse. Large-scale theatrical productions provide audiences with amazing talent shows, but smaller, more experimental events in unusual settings also provide them a new and creative way to experience dance. Everyone may enjoy dance, regardless of their financial situation, thanks to the numerous free performances that take place in public venues like the Place des Terreaux and the Parc de la Tête d'Or.

The Rencontres Chorégraphiques, a program devoted to up-and-coming dance talent, is one of the festival's most intriguing elements. This helps to foster the future of the art form by giving emerging choreographers and performers a priceless stage on which to present their work. In the center of Lyon, the Biennale de la Danse celebrates the force of dance, expression, and innovation with its varied program and broad appeal.

Lyon's Seasonal Events

Seasonal events on Lyon's yearly calendar offer distinctive opportunities to take advantage of the city's many attractions all year long and reflect its shifting rhythms. These activities, which range from summer festivals to winter markets, encapsulate the spirit of each season and enhance the allure of your trip.

In Lyon, Spring is characterized by flowering plants and lively outdoor activities. The old Roman theaters host a cultural event called Les

Nuits de Fourvière that combines dance, drama, music, and film. The hillside theater's stunning outdoor performances provide an experience that will never be forgotten. Another highlight is the Lyon Spring Fair, which takes place in late April and offers family-friendly events, artisanal crafts, and local produce. It's the ideal chance to sample the city's delectable cuisine and experience its vibrant environment.

Lyon is busiest during the summer season, when there are many outside activities. A well-liked summertime tradition in the city is the Open-Air Cinema Festival, when movies are screened in parks and other public areas, fostering a laid-back, neighborhood vibe. Lyon's Jazz Festival is another summertime highlight, offering free concerts and small-scale acts in the city center, frequently with the Rhône and Saône rivers as backdrops.

The Fête de la Gastronomie, a celebration of French culinary excellence, takes place in Autumn when the temperature cools. Visitors may enjoy the best Lyonnaise cuisine at special events, banquets, and seminars held at restaurants across the city. Foodies are invited to experience Lyon's cuisines and try new ones at this event.

Lastly, Lyon's Winter is a season of brightness and warmth, with the Place Carnot hosting the Marché de Noël (Christmas Market). The festive market is the ideal way to get into the Christmas season, complete with sparkling lights, mouth watering food, and handcrafted presents.

No matter when you visit Lyon, there will always be an interesting event or festival to take part in because every season offers something fresh. Lyon's festivals provide an unending array of cultural richness, from the spectacular lights of the Fête des Lumières to the exhilarating performances of the Biennale de la Danse. It is understandable why this city is regarded as one of France's most thriving and dynamic cultural centers.

SHOPPING

Lyon offers a shopping experience that is as stylish and varied as its rich cultural legacy, combining substance and elegance. Lyon offers something to fulfill any shopper's desire, whether they want to look for one-of-a-kind, handcrafted treasures or indulge in luxury goods. Lyon's retail scene is a voyage in and of itself, with its bohemian appeal of Croix-Rousse, its lively local markets full of regional treats, and its luxury stores along the streets of Presqu'île. As we examine the top shopping destinations in this chic French city, be ready to indulge in the ultimate kind of retail therapy.

Presqu'île Luxury Shopping

With a variety of upscale shops and designer boutiques that match the most stylish neighborhoods in Paris, Presqu'île is Lyon's luxury shopping destination for individuals who appreciate better things in life. Nestled between the Rhône and Saône rivers, this neighborhood is home to some of the city's most upscale retail establishments, including well-known French and international labels.

Commence your shopping expedition along Rue de la République, a magnificent street dotted with upscale shops and high-end merchants. Everything from traditional footwear from Christian Louboutin to timeless Parisian couture at Louis Vuitton can be found here. Hermès and Chanel also have their exquisite emporiums that provide the newest in luxury clothes, accessories, and perfumes if you're feeling really adventurous.

Make sure to visit the Galeries Lafayette department store, a French institution that combines luxury and French elegance under one roof, while you walk about the neighborhood. Here, you may find the ideal ensemble, a novel scent, or a striking piece of jewelry. In addition to fashion, Presqu'île has a superb assortment of upscale home goods and gourmet food stores, making it the ideal place to buy a present or indulge yourself.

Presqu'île is also home to a few art galleries and antique stores where you may purchase exquisite paintings, sculptures, and other works of art if you're an art enthusiast. Presqu'île is the ideal location for a chic shopping experience in Lyon because of its fashion, art, and luxury merchandise.

Croix-Rousse Boutique Shops

With a variety of boutique shops that radiate bohemian charm and regional flare, Croix-Rousse provides a more personal and varied shopping experience than Presqu'île's slick sophistication. Known for its artistic atmosphere and its past as Lyon's center for silk weaving, this hilltop neighborhood is reflected in its stores.

Small, independent stores dotting Croix-Rousse's winding lanes each have something special to offer. This is the spot to go if you're searching for unique fashion items that aren't available in the mainstream. You may peruse carefully chosen collections of apparel, jewelry, and accessories that are frequently handmade or locally produced, and designers display their products in simple settings.

You can search for unique treasures at the numerous vintage stores dotted around the area. The stores of Croix-Rousse are brimming with unique items, whether you're searching for vintage apparel, antique furniture, or unusual home décor. For individuals who like browsing through antique clothing, artwork, and memorabilia from various eras, the well-known vintage boutique La Caverne d'Ali Baba is a must-visit.

Visit one of the silk workshops that are still in operation in Croix-Rousse if you enjoy Lyon's rich silk history. While learning about the centuries-old methods that make Lyon the center of the world's silk trade, you can buy exquisite silk scarves, ties, and other items produced from the city's distinctive fabric. These stores provide a window into Lyon's workmanship and are the ideal fusion of modern design and tradition, allowing for an incredibly unique shopping experience.

Souvenirs and Local Markets

The city's local markets are a veritable gold mine of distinctive trinkets and regional specialties for anyone wishing to take a bit of Lyon home with them. Offering everything from handcrafted items to fresh vegetables, these bustling markets are an integral part of Lyon's culture and a great way to experience the lively ambiance of the city.

Commence at the Marché Saint-Antoine, which is situated beside the Saône River. Because of its exquisite assortment of fresh fruits, vegetables, cheeses, and meats, this outdoor market is a favorite among both locals and tourists. The region's culinary treats, such as charcuterie, quenelles (Lyon's signature dish), and freshly baked brioche, are sure to delight foodies. The market is also a great place to purchase regional specialties that are frequently handed down through the generations, like Lyon's renowned cooking tools or copper cookware.

Visit Le Marché de la Croix-Rousse for a more varied experience. There, you can discover a variety of products, from handcrafted jewelry to artisanal cheeses. The creative spirit of the neighborhood gives this market a rather bohemian character. It's also the perfect area to buy up gifts that represent Lyon's distinct cultural past, such as silk scarves, local pottery, or wonderfully produced leather products.

Visit Les Halles de Lyon-Paul Bocuse, an indoor market specializing in fine culinary goods, for something genuinely unique. This market, named for the renowned French chef

Paul Bocuse, is a foodie's dream come true. Some of the greatest local specialties, such as foie gras, truffles, fine chocolates, and wines, may be bought here. The quality of the products is unmatched, and many of the market's vendors are masters of their trade. It's a great spot to grab a treat for yourself or to discover a special present for a loved one.

Lyon's retail culture provides a fascinating blend of high-end couture, eccentric shops, and genuine local markets, regardless of your tastes. Every shopper may discover something genuinely unique in the city's varied retail areas, which showcase its combination of modern innovation and old-world elegance. Whether you're wandering through the high-end alleys of Presqu'île, discovering hidden jewels in Croix-Rousse, or seeking for regional specialties at the local markets, Lyon's shopping experience is as refined as it is varied.

TIPS FOR FAMILIES

Lyon is the perfect place for families who want to make enduring experiences together because of its captivating fusion of culture, history, and scenic beauty. From kids to parents and grandparents, this energetic metropolis has plenty to offer everyone in the family. Lyon promises to make your family trip a happy and memorable one, whether you're wandering through its lovely streets, dining on delectable food, or touring instructive museums. To help you get the most out of your trip, here are some family-friendly suggestions.

Attractions and Activities Suitable for Families

There are many family-friendly activities in Lyon that provide kids of all ages with both amusement and educational possibilities.

One of France's biggest and most exquisite urban parks, the Parc de la Tête d'Or, is the ideal place to begin your journey. There are several kid-friendly activities at this park, including a zoo with a variety of animals including giraffes, monkeys, and lions. The zoo is a great choice for families on a tight budget because it is entirely free. Families may have a picnic on the large lawns or take a leisurely stroll around the park's lakes, where pedal boats are available for rent, after seeing the animals. In addition, there are a number of playgrounds where kids can let off steam and a botanical garden that is ideal for teaching young children about the natural world.

The Musée des Confluences is a stunningly modern museum that combines science, anthropology, and natural history for a more hands-on experience. Children find the museum's interactive displays, which cover everything from space exploration to ancient animals, to be very captivating. With lots of chances for curiosity to grow, it's a fantastic environment for young brains to explore and learn.

The Mini World Lyon theme park, which features exquisitely detailed tiny landscapes, is another family favorite. This world of small delights will awe children with its little villages, railroads, and people. It's a captivating experience that piques curiosity and offers plenty of opportunities for family photos.

Consider taking your family to La Maison des Canuts, a museum honoring Lyon's illustrious silk-weaving past, if they like hands-on activities. Youngsters may even try their hand at weaving on a miniature loom and see live demonstrations of ancient silk-making processes. It's a great opportunity to engage children in something exciting and tactile while fostering a connection with the city's history.

Additionally, Lyon provides a variety of family-friendly tours that are certain to keep everyone occupied. Take a guided walking tour of the city's Traboules, the underground passages that were previously used as silk traders' routes. The enigmatic and ancient appeal of these intriguing tunnels and courtyards will enthrall both children and adults.

Restaurants That Are Kid-Friendly

You won't have to stress over finding a meal that the whole family will like when dining out in Lyon. The city's food culture is inviting and varied, with several eateries delivering the mouth watering delicacies Lyon is known for while also catering to younger palates.

Take the family to a classic bouchon, Lyon's hallmark restaurant style, for a genuinely local experience. The family-friendly bouchon Le Garet offers traditional Lyonnaise fare in a cozy setting. To make it simpler for the younger ones to experience real local flavors, their kid's menu has lighter versions of Lyon's well-known dishes, such as quenelles and gratin dauphinois.

Families will enjoy the more relaxed atmosphere and substantial, comforting food at Café des Fédérations. In the warmer months, they also provide outside seating so you can take advantage of Lyon's beautiful weather while enjoying some of the best cuisine the city has to offer. It's a great option for a family supper because the staff is kind and makes sure kids feel included.

Head to La Mère Jean, a welcoming, relaxed restaurant that specializes in regional cheeses, meats, and charcuterie, if your family wants something lighter or faster. Families may have a good lunch in a comfortable atmosphere thanks to the restaurant's intimate, rustic setting. In addition to enjoying the laid-back atmosphere of a family meal, the kids will adore sampling the various cheeses and cured meats.

There are also a number of family-friendly cafés in Lyon where you can relax with a dessert or coffee. The Vieux Lyon neighborhood's Le Bichat is a quaint café with many kid-friendly alternatives, including croissants, fresh juices, and basic sandwiches, making it the ideal place for a family break in between excursions.

Family-Friendly Outdoor Areas

Lyon is fortunate to have several outdoor areas that provide families with lots of chances to explore, unwind, and take in the city's natural beauty. Lyon's parks and riverbank promenades are great places for children to run, play, and get in touch with nature.

The Parc de Gerland, a large park on the banks of the Rhône River, is another fantastic green area to explore in addition to the Parc de la Tête d'Or. Large open areas for activities, a skate park for older kids, and a playground are all aspects of this park. It's a great place to have a family picnic or simply let the kids run about.

Lovely riverfront promenades that are ideal for a family stroll or bike ride can also be found at Lyon's Quais de Saône and Quais du Rhône. For a pleasant family adventure along the water, rent bikes or a tandem bike. Stop at one of the numerous shops lining the riverbanks for a snack or some ice cream. It's a wonderful opportunity to enjoy the city's beauty while exercising and enjoying some fresh air, and the vista is breathtaking.

A trip to Lyon's Jardin des Curiosités is a fascinating experience for families with smaller children. Perched atop a hill, this charming little garden has stunning city views and is a great location for a family portrait. Little ones will particularly like the garden's meandering paths and entertaining sculptures, which provide something to explore as you walk around.

Furthermore, Lyon's urban farms, such as La Ferme de la Tête d'Or, provide kids with the chance to engage with farm animals, making it the ideal day trip destination for families who like the outdoors. It's a great opportunity to have fun in an outdoor, interactive setting while teaching kids about the origins of their food.

There are several options to spend quality time with your loved ones, whether it's dining together, seeing a museum, or taking in Lyon's breathtaking natural scenery. Your family will feel completely at home while enjoying all that Lyon has to offer thanks to its pleasant ambiance, family-friendly activities, and mouthwatering food.

NIGHTLIFE

Lyon is transformed into a lively playground of excitement and vitality when the sun sets. Lyon has a lot to offer that will make your evening special, whether your preference is for a laid-back drink at a chic bar, dancing the night away at a hip nightclub, or taking part in cultural night activities. Lyon's nightlife is as varied and vibrant as the city itself, with its bustling atmosphere and international appeal. Here is a guide to some of Lyon's top nightlife options if you want to explore the city after dark.

Top Pubs & Bars

From stylish cocktail clubs to warm, rustic pubs, Lyon's bar scene is flourishing and offers a range of venues to suit every taste. You can find the ideal bar to relax in, whether your preference is to drink a perfectly created cocktail, savor a locally brewed beer, or just chill with a bottle of wine.

You should visit L'Antiquaire in Vieux Lyon if you enjoy cocktails. This chic pub with a speakeasy vibe is well known for its creative concoctions and cozy ambiance. L'Antiquaire provides an experience that is as much about the art of mixology as it is about unwinding, with a menu that combines traditional beverages with contemporary twists. It's the ideal location for a private date night or an elegant evening with friends.

Go to Le Sucre on the roof of the Hangar du Montolivet for something a little more relaxed. This pub, which is well-liked by both locals and visitors, is a terrific place to have a drink at sunset since it offers breathtaking views of the city. Live DJ performances are common throughout the warmer months, which enhances the vibrant atmosphere of the venue. For those seeking a relaxed yet exciting evening, Le Sucre is the ideal location because of its panoramic views, delectable cocktails, and laid-back vibe.

Don't miss Le Café des Fédérations in Presqu'île if you're craving something authentically French. It's a classic Lyonnais bouchon that turns into a welcoming bar at night. While conversing with locals and taking in the genuine ambiance of Lyon's nighttime scene, you may have a glass of Beaujolais wine or craft beer.

La Canute in Croix-Rousse is a fantastic choice for a more modern, alternative atmosphere. This little pub is well-known for its eclectic décor, inventive drinks, and laid-back, bohemian vibe. Local DJs play anything from lively dance tracks to more relaxed sounds, and the music is always spot on. It's the ideal spot to socialize with both locals and other tourists while enjoying a unique beverage.

Popular Clubs

There is something for every kind of night owl in Lyon's nightlife scene. Regardless of your musical preferences—electronic, indie rock, or hip-hop—the city has a nightclub that will have you dancing till the wee hours of the morning.

Le Ninkasi Kao is a must-see for fans of electronic music. With a varied schedule that includes techno, house, and everything in between, this enormous venue in the Gerland neighborhood is a center for live music and DJ sets. With a cutting-edge sound system and a large dance floor where you can immerse yourself in the sounds, the atmosphere is electrifying. Le Ninkasi Kao is the place to go if you want to have a fantastic night out.

Located in the Confluence neighborhood, La Sucrière is another well-known venue for electronic music. The raw, industrial vibe of this former warehouse turned club contributes to its allure. The most innovative sounds and a party-savvy audience can be found at La Sucrière, which is well-known for showcasing international DJs and themed events. The venue is one of Lyon's top nightlife attractions for fans of electronic music because of its large size and excellent acoustics.

The place to go if you want a more varied selection of genres is Le Transbordeur. Everything from hip-hop and electronic acts to rock and independent bands can be found at this legendary venue in the Villeurbanne neighborhood. The club is popular among both concertgoers and club members due to its amazing sound system and immersive stage setup. Whether you're here to dance to your favorite music or witness a live band, Le Transbordeur provides an exciting nighttime experience.

Visit Le Sonic for a more private, subterranean experience. This little venue, which is close to the Berges du Rhône, focuses on independent and live music performances. Music aficionados seeking a more genuine experience adore it for its raw, unpolished spirit and intimate environment, which allow for personal contact with the musicians. It's the ideal location to see up-and-coming artists and have a fun-filled evening.

Events for Cultural Nights

Lyon provides a wide range of cultural events and performances that come alive after dark, so it's not only about clubs and pubs. There are plenty of things to do when the sun sets if you want to take advantage of the city's diverse cultural attractions.

The Fête des Lumières (Festival of Lights), which takes place in December, is one of Lyon's most well-known cultural events. With light displays and creative installations strewn around Lyon's famous monuments, this amazing festival turns the city into a stunning canvas of color and light. Lyon attracts tourists from all over the world with its imaginative and breathtaking illumination of its streets, squares, and buildings. This is a must-see event that honors art and technology in the most spectacular way if you're ever in Lyon during the winter.

See a show at the Opéra de Lyon for a more conventional cultural experience. The city's commitment to the arts is demonstrated by the opera, ballet, and classical music concerts held at this historic location. The Opéra de Lyon provides a sophisticated and enlightening evening, whether you're taking in a world-class opera or a magnificent ballet performance.

With so many theaters showing everything from modern plays to traditional French theater, Lyon has a lot to offer theatergoers. One of the most prominent theaters in the city, Le Théâtre des Célestins is renowned for its small setting and top-notch plays. There is always something going on in this iconic location, with shows ranging from comedies to dramas.

The Nuits Sonores music festival, which takes place in May, is the last option if you're looking for something a little more participatory. A multi-day immersive experience for music enthusiasts, Nuits Sonores is a celebration of electronic music that takes over a variety of locations across Lyon, including cultural centers and industrial warehouses.

Lyon's nightlife has something for everyone, whether you want to dance, sip on a classy cocktail, or take in the city's vibrant cultural environment. You can always find the ideal way to spend your evening in this vibrant, creative city thanks to the diverse range of experiences and infectious enthusiasm.

ECO-FRIENDLY TOURING

Lyon, a city renowned for its rich history and lively culture, is also moving toward sustainability, which makes it a great place for tourists who care about the environment. Lyon provides a range of opportunities for tourists to experience the city while reducing their environmental effect thanks to its green initiatives, sustainable eating options, and dedication to encouraging eco-friendly transportation. Here are some important factors to take into account if you want to travel responsibly when visiting this vibrant French city. These can help you make more environmentally friendly decisions without sacrificing your enjoyment.

Sustainable Lodging

Where you stay is important when it comes to eco-friendly travel. From eco-friendly hotels to eco-aware boutique guesthouses, Lyon is home to an increasing range of lodging alternatives that are dedicated to lessening their environmental impact.

Hotel Silky by HappyCulture, a chic boutique hotel in the center of Lyon's Presqu'île neighborhood, is a prime example. The use of environmentally friendly cleaning supplies, energy-efficient lighting, and water-saving techniques are just a few examples of the hotel's commitment to sustainable practices. Visitors may take pleasure in a contemporary, pleasant stay with the knowledge that their lodging is contributing to lessening its environmental effect.

For individuals seeking a more opulent yet environmentally friendly solution, Villa Maia is a great pick. This five-star hotel, which blends eco-friendly principles with modern luxury, is located in the serene Fourvière neighborhood. It gets local, organic ingredients for its restaurant and spa, employs sustainable energy, and encourages waste reduction through recycling programs. For tourists who wish to have a comfortable but sustainable stay, this is the best choice.

The stunning boutique hotel La Cour des Loges, located in the Vieux Lyon district, offers an additional choice. This environmentally aware business utilizes trash reduction initiatives and energy-efficient technology to emphasize sustainability. Additionally, the hotel collaborates with regional producers to provide visitors with a taste of Lyon's delectable cuisine, emphasizing seasonal, organic, and local products. By staying here, you can support environmentally friendly travel while taking in the charms of Lyon's historic district.

Another great alternative for those on a tighter budget is Hostel Lyon. The hostel encourages visitors to make responsible decisions, such as using less energy while visiting, and takes pleasure in the use of eco-friendly materials in its design. The hostel's central location gives it a convenient starting point for exploring the city on foot or by bicycle, and the welcoming staff will offer advice on how to make the most of your environmentally aware stay.

Eco-Friendly Dining Choices

Sustainability isn't limited to your lodging; it also includes the food you consume. With many restaurants adopting organic, locally produced products and minimizing food waste, Lyon, known for its rich culinary legacy, provides a wide variety of eating alternatives that stress sustainability.

A notable example is La Tentation des Grands Ducs, a restaurant dedicated to sustainable practices with a cuisine that emphasizes seasonal and organic foods. This restaurant's chef takes pleasure in producing mouthwatering dishes that highlight the finest local ingredients while lessening their negative effects on the environment. The restaurant provides a great example of how eating can be both ecological and pleasurable by utilizing organic ingredients, helping out local farmers, and reducing food waste.

Le Bistrot de Lyon provides a fantastic sustainable eating experience for those looking for a farm-to-table experience. The cafe makes sure that everything it serves is local and fresh by sourcing the majority of its ingredients from neighboring farmers. It is the perfect option for guests who care about the environment because of their dedication to sustainability, which extends beyond the source of their food. They also utilize eco-friendly packaging and compost food waste.

Le Kitchen Café, a welcoming place that takes pleasure in utilizing sustainable, local, and organic ingredients, is another excellent choice.

The café offers a range of environmentally friendly and healthful alternatives on its menu, including freshly squeezed juices and plant-based meals. Le Kitchen Café provides a sustainable eating experience that benefits the environment and your health, whether you're searching for a small lunch or a substantial breakfast.

A must-see for individuals who would rather savor regional cuisine while reducing their environmental effect is Les Halles de Lyon Paul Bocuse. Many of the exhibitors at this famous food market prioritize ecological practices, such as using seasonal foods and reducing packaging waste, even though it is typically linked to excellent Lyonnaise cuisine. Spend some time perusing the market, which offers a wide variety of environmentally friendly food alternatives, and lend your support to local, sustainable manufacturers.

Consider dining at Ninkasi, a nearby brewery that uses organic ingredients and employs sustainable brewing methods, for a genuinely one-of-a-kind and environmentally friendly experience. Craft beer lovers will love Ninkasi because it blends sustainability with the city's beer culture, providing organic and locally made beer in a vibrant and eco-friendly setting.

Walking or Biking Around Lyon

Lyon is the ideal city to explore on foot or by bicycle because of its small size and dedication to sustainability. The city's bike-friendly streets, well-kept public areas, and designated bike lanes entice tourists to forgo driving and take advantage of a more environmentally responsible form of transportation.

The greatest approach to learn about Lyon's rich history and culture is to stroll through its quaint districts. It's best to explore the ancient Vieux Lyon neighborhood on foot, which has Renaissance buildings and winding cobblestone streets. While lowering your carbon footprint, take your time exploring the charming squares, stopping by the stunning churches, and shopping locally.

Another of France's bike-friendliest towns is Lyon. Biking is a fantastic way to see the city's many areas, and there is a vast network of bike lanes. There are many beautiful routes to explore when riding, whether you're through the Parc de la Tête d'Or or along the Saône

River. Lyon's bike-sharing program, Vélo'v, makes it simple for tourists to borrow bikes for quick excursions, enabling them to move between neighborhoods in an environmentally responsible manner. Additionally, there are a number of guided bike tours that highlight the city's historical and cultural sites, allowing you to learn while reducing your environmental effect.

Another environmentally friendly choice for individuals who would like to explore more slowly is Lyon's public transport system. The city provides an efficient, renewable energy-powered bus, tram, and metro system that is well-connected. An simple and environmentally responsible method to move around the city is to purchase a Lyon City Card, which gives you access to public transportation for the duration of your visit.

Lyon's dedication to sustainability is also evident in its urban areas, where green projects like green roofs and eco-friendly public parks can be found all around the city. Stop by the Parc de la Tête d'Or, one of France's biggest urban parks, or take a walk along the Rhône Riverbanks, both of which provide the ideal way to be outdoors without ever leaving the city.

You can support Lyon's dedication to sustainable tourism and have a memorable and enlightening time in one of France's most beautiful cities by choosing eco-friendly lodging, eating, and transportation. The finest aspect? Enjoying Lyon's cuisine, culture, and history while reducing your environmental impact will make your trip both pleasurable and conscientious.

USEFUL REFERENCE

Having the correct information is crucial when planning your trip to Lyon in order to guarantee a seamless, secure, and pleasurable visit. This area offers helpful guidance to help you move about the city with confidence, from health and safety recommendations to an awareness of local traditions. These suggestions can help you feel ready for your trip to Lyon, regardless of your level of experience.

Safety and Health Advice

Although Lyon is a rather secure city for visitors, it's still advisable to use common sense when traveling there. If you need help, there are several pharmacies and medical facilities in the city, which has a well-regarded healthcare system. The following are some crucial safety and health advice:

Make sure you have travel health insurance that covers unexpected medical expenses overseas. While the majority of EU travelers may get healthcare by using their European Health Insurance Card (EHIC), some might have to pay cash. Before you go, it is advisable to confirm your insurance coverage.

- Vaccinations: There are no specific vaccinations needed for travel to Lyon, however it's a good idea to ask your doctor for any latest advice. Vaccinations against tetanus, hepatitis A, and hepatitis B are often recommended for general travel.

- Pharmacies: A green cross outside makes it easy to identify pharmacies, which are common in Lyon. The majority of pharmacies give health advice, over-the-counter medications, and some even provide basic medical services. You won't have any problem locating a pharmacy if you ever need medical goods.

- Emergency Services: To contact police, fire, or ambulance services in an emergency, phone 112. In the EU, including France, this is the standard emergency number. You may reach the police at 17 and the fire department at 18 for non-emergencies.

- Safety: Although Lyon is regarded as a safe city, common sense warnings should be followed. Keep your possessions close at hand, particularly in busy places like tourist attractions or public transportation, and use ATMs with caution at night. After nightfall, stay on well-lit streets and stay away from remote regions if you're not acquainted with the area.

Regional Customs and Etiquette

Your contacts with locals might be more pleasant and kind if you are aware of their traditions and etiquette. Lyon locals are renowned for their warmth and friendliness, despite the French being noted for their formality and politeness. The following advice can help you deal with social situations in Lyon:

The customary French greeting between friends or acquaintances is a handshake or a courteous kiss on both cheeks (les bises). However, a handshake is more typical in formal or business settings. Depending on the time of day, it is usual to say "Bonjour" (good day) or "Bonsoir" (good evening) when you first meet someone.

- Table Manners Meals are often seen as social gatherings, and dining is a significant aspect of Lyon society. Always wait for the host to start eating before you do, and keep your hands on the table (but not your elbows) out of courtesy. It is usual to offer a little gift, such as wine or flowers, as a token of thanks when you are asked for lunch.

- Dress Code Compared to certain other nations, the French have a tendency to dress more formally. Even for informal occasions, individuals in Lyon often wear fashionable attire. Although there isn't a rigid dress requirement for visitors, it is appreciated when they are well-groomed and respectful, particularly when eating or visiting places of worship.

- Tipping: Tipping is not required in France since service is usually included by restaurant bills (search for "service compris"). If you were pleased with the service, it is usual to leave a tiny change (about 5–10%). It's also typical to round up the fee or leave a little tip for hotel employees or taxi drivers.

The French are renowned for having well-organized lines, particularly in establishments like bakeries and cafés. It's crucial to refrain from cutting in line and patiently wait your time. Respect for the inhabitants and their customs is shown by this.

Advice on Language and Interaction

Although Lyon's official language is French, many residents, particularly in the tourist districts, speak English to some degree. Building rapport with locals may be greatly aided by attempting to acquire a few simple French words. Here are some helpful linguistic pointers:

- Simple Expressions:
 "Bonjour" means "good day."
 "Merci" means "thank you," while "S'il vous plaît" means "please."
 "Excusez-moi" means "pardon me."
 - "Où est...?" (Where is it?)
 - "Combien ça coûte?" (What is the price?)
  "Je parle un peu de français" literally translates as "I speak a little French."

The French place a high importance on being courteous, so when you enter stores or restaurants, always say "Bonjour" or "Bonsoir" to customers. Saying "Au revoir" (Goodbye) after departing is also usual.

Learning Basic words Although English is often spoken in tourist locations, particularly in restaurants, hotels, and museums, knowing a few essential French words will improve your visit and make you more popular with the locals. Basic expressions like "Pouvez-vous m'aider?" (Can you assist me?) or even "Parlez-vous anglais?" It would be extremely appreciated if you could speak English.

- Communication: Although they may come off as reticent, French people are typically kind. Particularly in formal settings, it's critical to maintain deference and avoid being too familiar. But the people of Lyonnais are kind and open once you break the ice.

Contacts for Emergencies

It's always a good idea to be ready for any emergency while traveling. The following is a list of crucial emergency contacts and helpful phone numbers you may need when traveling:

In the event of a police, fire, or medical emergency, dial 112. Throughout the EU, including France, this is the European emergency number.

- Police: For prompt help with police-related matters, contact 17.

- Fire Department: Call 18 if you need fire or rescue services. You may reach the local fire department, which can also handle some medical situations, by calling this number.

- Ambulance: To summon an ambulance in the event of an emergency, dial 15. Many pharmacies in Lyon supply over-the-counter drugs and also give assistance for non-urgent medical issues.

- Lost Property: You may check with the authorities at 17 or the local Lost Property Office at the Lyon Tourist Office if you lose anything while visiting Lyon.

- Pharmacies: There are pharmacies all across Lyon for minor medical concerns. The majority of pharmacies offer employees who can help you with prescription, guidance, and basic first aid supplies and who speak a rudimentary form of English.

Embassy Contacts: You may get in touch with the embassy of your home country if you misplace your passport or want consular help.

For instance, several nations have their own consular services in France, and the U.S. Consulate in Lyon is the gateway to the U.S. embassy.

Having these useful facts at your fingertips will guarantee a stress-free and pleasurable journey to Lyon. Be prepared at all times, and keep in mind that Lyon residents are kind and willing to help if you need it while there. Now that you have these pointers, you are prepared to experience this amazing city's beauty and culture to the fullest!

SAMPLE ITINERARIES

With its lively culture, rich history, and charm, Lyon has much to offer all kinds of tourists. You may customize your trip to fit your interests, whether you're going for a day trip or a weeklong getaway. Here are three suggested itineraries that will help you get the most out of your stay in Lyon, from the must-see sights to a comprehensive, immersive experience.

Lyon's One-Day Highlights

This one-day itinerary will take you through the most famous locations and attractions in Lyon while encapsulating its charm if you're pressed for time but still want to see the best of the city.

- Morning: Take a walk around the city's UNESCO World Heritage-listed Vieux Lyon (Old Lyon) neighborhood to start your day. Start in Vieux Lyon's main plaza, Place Saint-Jean, and explore its winding cobblestone alleyways. Spend some time admiring the stunning Saint-Jean Cathedral, which is renowned for its astronomical clock, and its Renaissance architecture. Discover

Lyon's secret passages, known as the Traboules, which have been utilized for generations to go between buildings and around courtyards.

- Late Morning: After taking in Vieux Lyon's historic ambience, go to the Basilica of Notre-Dame de Fourvière, which is situated on a hill with a view of the city. The Funicular takes you to the top, or you may walk up via the twisting streets. With its elaborate interior and expansive terrace views of Lyon, the basilica itself is a stunning sight on the inside as well as the outside. Remember to visit the Fourvière Hill gardens for a serene time and breathtaking sweeping views.

- Lunch: Visit one of Lyon's well-known Bouchons, which are classic Lyonnaise eateries that provide substantial regional fare. For a genuine experience, try Bouchon Le Jura or Le Café des Fédérations. Choose regional specialties such as salade lyonnaise, quenelles (a kind of fish dumpling), and, of course, a glass of Beaujolais wine.

- Afternoon: After lunch, stroll a little to one of France's most prominent art museums, the Musée des Beaux-Arts. Explore its vast collection, which includes both ancient and modern artwork, for about an hour. It is located in a stunning former convent. After seeing the museum, take a leisurely walk to the Place des Terreaux, a public plaza where you may look at the magnificent Bartholdi Fountain.

- Late afternoon: Make your way to one of France's biggest urban parks, the Parc de la Tête d'Or. Explore the park's vast gardens, tranquil lake, and lovely rose garden by taking a leisurely stroll or renting a bike. Visit the Lyon Zoo in the park if you have time, or just unwind by the lake.

- Evening: Have a leisurely meal in the Presqu'île neighborhood as your last destination of the day. Explore foreign selections or choose from a range of eateries serving Lyon's famous cuisine. Enjoy a drink at a café with a view of the Saône River and the city skyline lighted as you cap off your evening.

Plan for a Weekend Getaway

You will have enough opportunity to discover some of Lyon's hidden treasures and take your time exploring the city's major attractions during your two days there. This trip includes visits to historical sites, cultural events, and an opportunity to savor Lyon's cuisine.

Day 1: Lyon's History and Gastronomic Pleasures

Morning - Vieux Lyon - Begin your day by seeing the Saint-Jean Cathedral and the quaint streets of the Renaissance. For a taste of Lyon's intriguing history, visit Musée Gadagne, home of the Museum of the History of Lyon. Explore the traboules from here to learn about the history and architecture of Lyon.

Lunch: Savor a lunch at a neighborhood bouchon to try some of the delicacies of Lyonnaise cuisine. Enjoy a glass of Côtes du Rhône wine, which is made in the surrounding area, with your meal.

- Afternoon: Take the funicular or hike up the hill to the Basilica of Notre-Dame de Fourvière in the afternoon. After that, go a little distance to the Roman Theaters of Fourvière to see the remains of Lyon, once known as Lugdunum, a significant Roman city.

- Evening: For supper, visit the Presqu'île neighborhood, which offers a variety of eateries. After that, take a stroll along the Saône River to Place Bellecour, one of Europe's biggest public squares, which is lit up at night and provides fantastic city views.

Day 2: Leisure and Culture

- Morning: Visit the Musée des Beaux-Arts to start your day and be surrounded by artwork from across the ages. After that, take in the magnificent architecture of Hôtel de Ville (City Hall) and explore Place des Terreaux.

- Lunch: Savor lunch in Les Halles de Lyon Paul Bocuse, one of Lyon's bustling local markets. You may enjoy local cheeses, meats, fish, and fresh veggies here.

Spend the day at the Parc de la Tête d'Or, where you may explore the lovely gardens, go to the zoo, or take a boat ride on the lake.

- Evening: Visit La Croix-Rousse, a hilltop district renowned for its artisan stores and bohemian vibe, to round out your tour. Have supper at one of the neighborhood eateries and cap off the evening with libations at a café with a view of the city.

A Week in Lyon: Comprehensive Study

You have more than enough time to really explore Lyon throughout a week, delving into its history, culture, and cuisine. For those who want to discover Lyon's genuine spirit, here is a suggested itinerary.

Day 1: Vieux Lyon and Arrival

When you get to Lyon, take your time getting settled. Explore the Saint-Jean Cathedral and the traboules, get your first taste of Lyonnaise cuisine, and spend the day strolling about Vieux Lyon.

Day 2: Roman Lyon and Fourvière Hill

To learn more about Lyon's Roman past, explore the Basilica of Notre-Dame de Fourvière and the Roman Theaters before continuing your exploration at the Musée Gallo-Romain.

Day 3: Culture and Art

Visit the Musée des Beaux-Arts for the day before continuing on to the Musée des Confluences, a remarkable museum of science and anthropology situated at the meeting point of the Rhône and Saône rivers. The museum is worth seeing only for its futuristic architecture.

Day 4: Culinary Delights and Markets

Explore some of Lyon's most renowned bouchons for lunch after spending the morning at Les Halles de Lyon Paul Bocuse. To discover more about the city's culinary heritage, enroll in a cooking class or a guided food tour in the afternoon.

Day 5: Shopping and the Park de la Tête d'Or

After spending the morning in Parc de la Tête d'Or, spend the afternoon shopping on the Presqu'île. Because Lyon is famed for producing silk, be sure to visit the silk stores for one-of-a-kind mementos.

Day 6: Visit Perouges or Beaujolais for the day

Visit Perouges, a medieval town near Lyon, or go wine tasting in the Beaujolais wine region for a day excursion.

Day 7: Croix-Rousse Exploration and Departure

Spend your last day in the La Croix-Rousse neighborhood, taking in the distinctive ambiance, neighborhood marketplaces, and expansive views of Lyon. Before you leave for the train station or airport, take one more walk along the Rhône River while you think back on your week.

There are several ways to explore Lyon's history, culture, and exceptional cuisine, regardless of how long you intend to stay or how long you're staying. Every one of these itineraries will guarantee that you depart with a greater comprehension of what makes this extraordinary city so unique.

CONCLUDING REMARKS & SUGGESTIONS

Lyon is a city that invites visitors to explore, discover, and fall in love with its charms because of its unique combination of history, culture, and food. Here are some last ideas and suggestions to make sure your stay in Lyon has been as remarkable as the city itself as you get ready to wrap up your journey to this energetic French treasure. These insights, which include must-do activities and insider advice from locals, will motivate you to make the most of your time in this amazing place—and maybe even arrange your return.

Experiences You Must Have

Every kind of tourist may find something unique in Lyon's many renowned experiences and hidden treasures. A few experiences are definitely necessary to grasp the city's actual spirit, even if the major attractions are well worth your time:

- Discover Vieux Lyon: With its lovely streets and Renaissance architecture, Lyon's Old Town is an outdoor museum. This neighborhood provides a thorough exploration of Lyon's rich past, whether you want to explore the winding lanes or take in the splendor of the Saint-Jean Cathedral. Don't miss the Traboules, secret passages that Lyon's citizens have been using for years.

The Basilica of Notre-Dame de Fourvière is worth a visit. This famous basilica, which is perched on a hilltop, provides amazing views of the city and beautiful architecture. The surrounding gardens and ancient structures are just as intriguing as the Funicular ride up to the basilica, which is a pleasure in and of itself.

- Taste Lyonnaise food: Lyon is regarded as France's culinary capital, so sampling the regional food is a must. Try specialties like quenelles, salade lyonnaise, and andouillette sausage as you visit a traditional bouchon. Savor the tastes that make Lyon one of the world's top culinary destinations by pairing your meal with a glass of wine from the surrounding Beaujolais area.

- Walk Through Parc de la Tête d'Or: One of France's biggest urban parks, this vast space has plenty to offer everyone. It's the ideal location to relax and enjoy Lyon's natural beauty, with its tranquil lakes, verdant parks, and zoo.

Explore Modern Lyon at La Confluence: If you have an interest in architecture and urban planning, you should definitely check out the La Confluence neighborhood. With its futuristic architecture, cutting-edge museums like the Musée des Confluences, and lively riverside areas that inspire you to unwind and think, this neighborhood is a breathtaking example of contemporary city design.

- Take a Cooking Class: Enroll in a cooking class where you may learn to make classic Lyonnaise meals if you want to fully immerse yourself in Lyon's culinary culture. Getting your hands dirty in the kitchen is the best way to experience the city's culinary culture.

Locals' Inside Advice

Connecting with the city and its residents is more important while visiting Lyon than just taking in the attractions. The people are renowned for their friendliness and kindness, and they have offered some insider advice to help you have an even more amazing trip:

While Lyon's major attractions are unmissable, don't forget to check out the lesser-known areas of the city as well. Visit the Croix-Rousse neighborhood, which has small stores, bohemian cafés, and stunning views of Lyon. With so many silk stores and studios to tour, the neighborhood also provides intriguing insights into the city's history of silk weaving.

- Avoid Rushing Through Meals: Dining in Lyon is an experience rather than a passing visit. In addition to enjoying the chat that goes along with their meals, locals take their time. Plan to linger over your meal and savor the occasion, whether you're dining at a Michelin-starred restaurant or enjoying a more formal lunch at a bouchon.

- Explore Lyon's marketplaces: The city's gastronomic culture is reflected in Lyon's marketplaces. Take advantage of the opportunity to explore Les Halles de Lyon Paul Bocuse, a thriving food market that is a foodie's paradise. The best cheeses, meats, and pastries are available at the booths, making it the ideal location to try the freshest foods or bring home delectable mementos.

Experience the Saône and Rhône Rivers by Boat: There are many options for leisurely boat cruises since Lyon is situated where two rivers converge. Cruise the Rhône River at sunset aboard a Bateau Mouche for a very unique experience. It's the ideal opportunity to take in the breathtaking skyline and architecture of the city from a new angle.

Accept the "Art of Living" in Lyon: Lyon is about living life to the fullest, not simply about history and cuisine. The city effortlessly combines luxury, leisure, and culture. Take some time to appreciate the laid-back and friendly atmosphere of the city, whether you're people-watching in Place Bellecour, drinking coffee at a neighborhood café, or taking in the art exhibits in the city's galleries.

You Must Attend Lyon's Festivals: You're in for a treat if you're traveling to Lyon during one of its numerous yearly events, including the Fête des Lumières (Festival of Lights) or Nuits Sonores (Music Festival). These activities are enthusiastically welcomed by the locals and provide a terrific opportunity to explore the creative energy of the city. If at all possible, schedule your visit around one of these exciting events by looking at the festival calendar.

Making Plans to Go Back to Lyon

There is little doubt that you will want to go back to Lyon following your stay. Lyon has a way of winning your heart and leaving you feeling deeply grateful for all it has to offer, from its historical treasures to its gastronomic pleasures, contemporary inventions, and lively cultural scene.

Stay Longer Next Time: If you have just been in Lyon for a few days, think about coming back for a longer stay. Beyond the popular tourist destinations, there's a ton more to explore, and you'll learn something new every time you go back. Maybe next time, arrange a day excursion to one of the surrounding locations, such as the medieval hamlet of Perouges or the Beaujolais wine region.

- Seasonal Visits: Depending on the time of year, Lyon provides different experiences. The city comes alive in the spring with beautiful gardens and outdoor activities. The parks and riverbanks are ideal for outdoor gatherings and picnics throughout the summer. The city's vineyards shine golden in the autumn, and the winter months are enchanted, particularly when the streets are illuminated by the Fête des Lumières. Depending on whatever season most interests you, schedule your return.

- Discover More About the Culinary Scene in Lyon: For foodies, Lyon is a haven, and there's always more to explore. If you've liked the wine and bouchons in the city, you may want to come back and explore the food scene more. To learn more about the cuisine that makes Lyon so well-known, schedule a cooking lesson, go on a culinary tour, or visit the local markets.

- Stay in Different Neighborhoods: To experience more of Lyon, think about staying in a different area on your way back. Every part of Lyon has its own distinct personality, from the artistic atmosphere of La Croix-Rousse to the historical charm of Vieux Lyon to the contemporary vitality of La Confluence.

With its alluring mix of culture, history, and fine dining, Lyon is a city that makes an impact on everyone who comes. Lyon will always have something fresh to offer, whether it's your first or fifth visit, and it's always waiting to welcome you back.

CONTACTS AND RESOURCES

You must have access to trustworthy resources while planning your trip to Lyon in order to maximize your experience. Having the correct tools may improve your experience and guarantee that your trip goes well, whether you're searching for skilled tour guides, current travel information, or useful maps and guides. We've put together a list of some of the top contacts and resources in this area to help you organize your trip to Lyon.

Official Websites for Travel

The official tourist websites provide a wealth of information for planning your trip. From restaurant listings and lodging suggestions to event calendars and travel advice, they provide a multitude of information. These websites will help you remain up to date on the latest events in Lyon and provide a one-stop shop for all the information you want.

The Official Website of Lyon Tourism
    For further information on Lyon, see the official tourist website (www.lyon-france.com).

Along with helpful travel advice, this website offers a thorough rundown of Lyon's food options, cultural events, and sights. For the most recent information on things to do, places to stay, and how to get about, it's the go-to source.

City Card of Lyon

The Lyon City Card website (www.lyoncitycard.com) is a vital resource for tourists who want to see the city's main sights. The card provides free or reduced admission to a number of museums, cultural landmarks, and public transit. It's a fantastic opportunity to explore some of Lyon's must-see sites at a reduced cost.

Métropole Lyon

The Lyon Métropole website (www.lyonmetropole.fr) offers information on neighboring locations in the Lyon area, such as wine tours, day excursions, and outdoor pursuits, for people who want to go outside of Lyon. If you want to visit the historic hamlet of Pérouges or the stunning Beaujolais wine area, this is the ideal resource.

These official websites are trustworthy tools for all of your planning requirements since they are updated often with fresh information.

Suggested Tour Companies

Lyon boasts a number of top-notch tour companies if you want guided tours or want someone with local knowledge to assist you get about the city. These businesses provide immersive experiences led by informed residents who can give insights into Lyon's history, culture, and culinary traditions, whether you're interested in guided bike rides, historical excursions, or cuisine tours.

A range of guided excursions, both private and group, are available from the Lyon Tourism Office. These trips include everything from historical tours of Vieux Lyon to gastronomic experiences in the city's renowned markets. These excursions provide a closer connection to Lyon as they are conducted by local guides who tell engaging tales about the city's history and present. For additional information and to make a reservation, visit their website.

Bike Tours with Lyon"

Lyon Bike Tours is a great choice if you wish to visit Lyon while riding a bicycle. With an emphasis on places like the Parc de la Tête d'Or and the Saône River, they provide bike excursions across the city. For those who prefer a more active approach to seeing the city while learning about its history and culture, this operator is ideal since it offers bike rentals and personalized excursions.

A range of culinary trips are available for food enthusiasts via Taste of Lyon. This tour operator takes you on a culinary adventure through Lyon's varied culinary scene, from classic bouchon restaurants to neighborhood markets like Les Halles de Lyon. Tours are intended to provide guests a better knowledge of Lyon's culinary culture by introducing them to the city's well-known specialties, such as quenelles, salade lyonnaise, and charcuterie.

Personalized walking tours that are catered to your interests are available from In Lyon Tours. In Lyon Tours offers a personalized and individualized experience, whether your goal is to see the city's galleries of modern art, discover the history of silk production in the city, or explore the Traboules. For those seeking a personalized and distinctive trip, this is the perfect option since their knowledgeable guides may customize the schedule to your interests.

These tour companies are well acclaimed for their expertise and professionalism, and their trips provide a more thorough understanding of Lyon's history, culture, and culinary scene. It is strongly advised to make reservations in advance, particularly during busy times.

Guides and Maps

Navigating Lyon may be a snap if you have trustworthy maps and instructions. Even though Lyon is a very accessible city, having a decent map will make it easier to navigate and guarantee that you don't miss any of the city's hidden treasures. The following tools will assist you in organizing your time in the city:

- Map of Lyon City
A free Lyon City Map is available at the Lyon Tourist Office and other tourist information locations across the city. Major landmarks, public transit lines, and important areas including Vieux Lyon, Presqu'île, and La Croix-Rousse are marked on these comprehensive and user-friendly maps. To

make planning your day easier, many maps also indicate places to eat, shop, and have fun.

- Mobile Apps Available for Download
You may easily traverse the city with the aid of a number of smartphone applications. Current information about walking routes and public transit may be found on Citymapper and Google Maps. Another excellent tool is the Lyon City Card App, which lets you keep track of the attractions you've been to and provides extra savings and deals while you're there.

A Guide to the Lonely Planet Lyon
Lonely Planet provides a thorough travel guide to Lyon for those who would rather have a hard copy. Along with helpful advice on where to stay, dine, and buy, this handbook offers comprehensive details on the city's history, sights, and culinary scene. For tourists who like to have everything they need in one location, it is a vital resource. Lonely Planet guides are renowned for their comprehensiveness and current suggestions.

Additionally, the Lyon Tourist Office offers a number of pamphlets that emphasize various facets of the city, including walking tours, bike routes, and gastronomic experiences. Both the official website and tourist information centers provide these pamphlets for download. They are especially beneficial for those who want advice or suggestions tailored to their hobbies.

In addition to making around Lyon easier, having these maps and guides at your disposal will guarantee that you don't miss any of the city's hidden gems that contribute to its distinctiveness.

Concluding Remarks

Your vacation to Lyon will be a memorable one if you have the proper tools. Lyon has a multitude of resources to assist you in organizing and navigating your trip, ranging from official tourist websites and knowledgeable tour operators to maps and in-depth publications. These connections can help you make the most of your stay in Lyon, a vibrant and culturally diverse city, whether you're looking for insider knowledge, local knowledge, or user-friendly resources.

Printed in Great Britain
by Amazon